PARTICIPANT
JOURNAL **THREE**

SEASONS OF HOPE

M. Donna MacLeod

To Erynne Lee MacLeod,
a cherished child
who loved Jesus
and now lives with him.

Scripture quotations contained herein are from the *New Revised Standard Version* of the Bible, copyright © 1993 and 1989, by the Division of Christian Education of the National Council of the Churches of Christ in the U.S.A., and are used by permission. All rights reserved.

Quotations from the English translation of the *Catechism of the Catholic Church* for the United States of America, copyright © 1994, United States Catholic Conference, Inc.—*Libreria Editrice Vaticana* are used by permission.

© 2007 by M. Donna MacLeod, RN, MSN

All rights reserved. No part of this book may be used or reproduced in any manner whatsoever except in the case of reprints in the context of reviews, without written permission from Ave Maria Press®, Inc., P.O. Box 428, Notre Dame, IN 46556.

Founded in 1865, Ave Maria Press is a ministry of the Indiana Province of Holy Cross.

www.avemariapress.com

ISBN-10 1-59471-114-3   ISBN-13 978-1-59471-114-5

Cover and text design by John Carson.

Printed and bound in the United States of America.

Contents

SEASON THREE

"*Seasons of Hope* Prayer" 5
Welcome to the *Participant Journal* 7
Session 1: Point of Departure 9
   Guidepost
   Home Journal: *Doubting Thomas* 12
Session 2: Path to Understanding 17
   Guidepost
   Home Journal: *Open Doors* 20
Session 3: Obstacles on the Journey 25
   Guidepost
   Home Journal: *Crippled Spirit* 28

Session 4: Path to Inner Healing 33
  Guidepost
  Home Journal: *Blind Faith* 36

Session 5: Way of Suffering 41
  Guidepost
  Home Journal: *Christ's Example* 44

Session 6: Final Destination 49
  Guidepost
  Home Journal: *No Tears* 52

Appendix
  Helpful Resources 56
  Network Directory 58
  Guide to Group Etiquette 60
  Season Three Survey 61

Acknowledgments 63

"Seasons of Hope Prayer"

Our Father,
in this season of sorrow,
we turn to you.
Weakened with sadness,
we shed tears beyond number.
May those you send to help us
bring your love and consolation.

In this season of sorrow,
we lift up our broken hearts to you.
Heal us with your tender mercy and
make this a season of hope.
Trusting in your infinite kindness,
we ask this of you
with the Son and the Holy Spirit.
Amen.

Welcome to the Participant Journal

Dear Brothers and Sisters in Christ Jesus,

When your loved one went home to the Lord, did you think that God was calling you to a new life in him, too? And that this new life held much more than pain and sorrow?

I had no idea what lay ahead when my daughter Erynne died. Years of caring for the dying and their families as a nurse did not prepare me for my own grief. Yet God would use the lessons I learned for the good of others. From the loss of a precious child a Christ-centered ministry to the bereaved and a hospice were born. God plans ahead. He didn't forget me, my family, or my community, and he hasn't forgotten you. He wants to console you.

Trusting in God and coming to the *Seasons of Hope* program blesses you in untold ways. The support of others who know what you go through is the first of many of God's gifts of love. Your broken heart will mend as your spirit lifts. I've seen it happen time and again.

A bible and this *Participant Journal* are all you need for the group sessions of *Seasons of Hope*. A group prayer begins the booklet and each session. Each week the facilitator will have you open to the Guidepost page for the theme, scripture citation, and activity to do before faith sharing begins.

The rest of the weekly journal is for you to use at home after the session. It generally takes about twenty minutes to complete the weekly homework—a commitment that most schedules can handle. If possible, find a quiet corner that is free of distractions. A good way to get focused is to read the week's Bible passage.

The opening comments in Looking Back give a fresh way to view the scripture story. The spiritual journey that began in the group session continues as you ask for guidance with A Prayer to Find the Way. You will read Steps Along the Path to learn how the scripture story relates to mourning and then spend time with the Reflection section to consider your situation. You can write your thoughts in the space provided under the heading, Journal Entry.

To help you cope, Moving Forward offers a Church tradition or an act of charity that generates hope. You finish the weekly journey with the Closing Prayer thanking God for the gift of consolation.

The end of the booklet has treasures of its own. Are you interested in literature and Web sites about losing a loved one? Check out Helpful Resources. Need a place to record contact information about your new friends at *Seasons of Hope*? Use the Network Directory. How about ground rules for the group? That's covered in Guide to Group Etiquette. Want to help your facilitators plan for the next season? The Season Three Survey lets you formally share your ideas.

With *Participant Journal* homework, you privately bring the trials of your loss to the Lord. You embrace his teachings, reflect on your loss, and share the painful moments so that your wounded spirit can grow strong in Christ.

May this unique way of placing Jesus Christ at the center of your grief bring you consolation.

In Christ,
M. Donna MacLeod

Session ONE

Guidepost: Point of Departure

Theme of the first session:

Believing

Scripture: John 20:24–29

🍃 Marking the Route

Exercise:

Please complete these statements in your cluster group:

- My name is _____.

- The rules about dealing with death that I remember from childhood are . . .

- The person who laid down the rules was _____ _____.

- The rules taught me that God . . .

 **Session ONE**

Notes

Home Journal: Point of Departure

Looking Back: *Doubting Thomas*

This week in group session we heard John 20:24–29 in which one of Jesus' disciples is tagged with the unenviable name of "Doubting Thomas." Some would argue that Thomas's reaction was appropriate. After all, his brethren claimed that Jesus was alive after his crucifixion and death on the cross. The grieving disciples sounded like they had lost their minds.

Had Thomas forgotten that Jesus had foretold his death and resurrection? Or had witnessing Christ's passion and death weakened the disciple's belief in him? What we know is that Jesus believed in Thomas. He understood grief, his followers, and their limitations. Addressing Thomas's doubt directly, Jesus offered his holy wounds for probing so that Thomas would believe. He used Thomas's shaken faith to send a message of healing to all who struggle to believe in him during mourning.

Instead of inflicting more pain on the Lord by touching his wounds, Thomas said, "My Lord and my God!" Some call those words the most explicit statement of faith in the New Testament. Thomas showed us that saints don't have to be perfect. They simply must love God.

# Session ONE   13

A Prayer to Find the Way

O merciful Savior,
in the troubled moments
since losing my loved one,
I have been afraid of many things.
Yet, like Thomas,
my love for you remains.
Through your kindness,
may the gift of faith
guide me through mourning.
Amen.

Steps Along the Path

Who hasn't had a moment of doubt after losing a loved one? Be comforted in knowing that when the resurrected Jesus finally encountered Thomas, he greeted him and the other mourners with "Peace be with you." The Prince of Peace didn't want their hearts to be troubled or afraid, so he came to them.

During this time of sorrow, have you thought about the many ways the Prince of Peace is present to you?

Reflection

One way to encounter Christ is to focus on an image of his sacred wounds. A picture of the crucified Christ from a book or prayer card will do, or sit before a crucifix in a church or chapel where you can gaze at a life-size figure. The wounds on Christ's hands, feet, and side represent the Lord's selfless act of love for all the saints and sinners of the ages.

Session ONE

Journal Entry

As Christians, we live with the expectation that when our time comes to an end, we will meet Jesus face-to-face. Sometimes being at the side of a dying loved one forces us to wrestle with our own mortality. That's perfectly normal. Also when we mourn the loss of a loved one, thoughts about life after death may arise.

Write down your thoughts about life after death. If you need a little help getting the words down, consider these opening phrases:

- Lord, losing _____, makes me realize . . .

- My connection to _____ has shown me that life is . . .

Moving Forward

Jesus surrounded himself with ordinary people with human weaknesses and gave them the means to be holy. Since the eleventh century, the Church has beatified or canonized saints to show heroic virtue worthy of public veneration.

Yet we are all called to lead holy lives. Living saints are simply all those who live according to the law God has given us. Our family members, friends, and those who dedicate their lives to God are among us every day.

This week honor your loved one by a visit to the grave. While you are there, remember something he or she used to do that reminds you of Christ.

Closing Prayer

O Savior of my soul,
with a grateful heart I thank you
for the gift of my departed loved one.
Strengthen my faith and let me recognize your face
as we walk this journey of sorrow together.
Amen.

Session TWO

Guidepost: Path to Understanding

Theme of the second session:
Knock and the Door Shall Be Opened
Scripture: Matthew 7:7–11

Marking the Route

Exercise:

1. Sketch Jesus at your door or conjure up that image in your mind's eye and describe what you see.

2. Ask Jesus for something you want that will ease your grief.

 Session TWO

Notes

Home Journal: Path to Understanding

Looking Back: *Open Doors*

Matthew 7:7–11 gives us a sense of how Jesus admires the kindness of God the Father. The Lord assures us that all prayers receive attention and are answered in the most loving manner. Yet the sorrow of losing a loved one may cause us to pause at that notion. Haven't we prayed for a cure for someone or for relief of someone's pain or for God to rescue someone from the jaws of death? And how often has the answer been no?

Jesus is adamant, though. "Ask, and it will be given you; search, and you will find . . . ." Is he telling us to seek truth? Can we ever break free of our tunnel vision and get a glimpse of God's wisdom?

Session TWO

A Prayer to Find the Way

O merciful Savior,
you teach us about God the Father's
infinite love and wisdom.
Let us discover him through you
as the door of consolation opens for
us.
Amen.

Steps Along the Path

Sometimes after a loss, grief is so confusing you may forget that God wants to console you. When you find it difficult to concentrate, to organize your thoughts, or to remember the simplest things, how can you pray? A wandering mind can't fully comprehend the message of a scripture passage, either. Once the initial confusion wears off, the impact of the loss may leave you deaf and blind to God's presence in your sorrow.

When you knock on God's door with prayer, do you recognize his reply? Quiet your own thoughts and listen attentively to what comes to mind. Try to imagine your request from God's perspective. For whose will to be done do you pray?

Jesus promises that our heavenly Father's gifts exceed our expectations and that his way is the way of perfect love and wisdom. His door opens to those who seek him.

Reflection

Jesus spent much of his ministry explaining the nature of God the Father and the loving regard he has for his creations. Your attitude toward God influences how you pray. Is it as expectant and trusting as Jesus recommends? Do you wonder if you are heard or whether the door of mercy will open for you? Reflect on your relationship with God. The better you know him, the better you will see God acting in your life. What do you think God's will is for you during these difficult days?

Session TWO

Journal Entry

In Matthew's account, Jesus speaks confidently about God the Father's desire to answer our prayers. Trust is the underlying issue. Jesus calls upon us to accept his advice and rely on his character, ability, strength, and truthfulness.

Write to Jesus about your trust in him and how it affects your prayer life, especially when doors need to be opened in times of trial.

Moving Forward

The path to understanding grief takes you past many entrances that promise spiritual growth. Attending a Christ-centered support group such as *Seasons of Hope* can map the way. You get to choose which door to knock on.

To knock takes a deliberate act on your part. One way to grow in the spirit is to stop by the doors of the tabernacle at your church. The sacred place of reservation that holds the hosts consecrated during Mass gives constant access to the presence of the Lord Jesus. The posture you assume (whether you kneel or sit in reverent attentiveness) will convey your heartfelt message to him as well.

If possible, spend quiet time there this week. Let your prayer knock for you, and expect the door of understanding to open wide.

Closing Prayer

Lord Jesus,
your words of encouragement
bring peace to my weary heart.
I'm grateful for the doors you open
for me.
Amen.

Session THREE

Guidepost: Obstacles on the Journey

Theme of the third session:

Our Infirmities

Scripture: Luke 13:10–13

Marking the Route

Exercise:

Think about how it will feel when the Lord heals your wounded spirit. Jot down your thoughts.

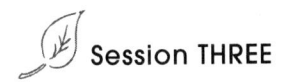

Notes

Home Journal: Obstacles on the Journey

Looking Back: *Crippled Spirit*

The backdrop for the story of Luke 13:10–13 contributes to its drama. It was the Sabbath—the seventh day of the week in the Hebrew calendar. Observed from Friday evening to Saturday evening, it is set aside for worship and rest from ordinary everyday activity. Jesus was at a synagogue, a house of worship, where his brethren gathered for the public reading of scripture, prayer and the sacrifice of praise, and instruction on religious matters.

After the reading, it was common for a synagogue leader to invite someone who was particularly qualified to speak to the congregation. That may be why Jesus was teaching that day before a crowd, which included a synagogue leader.

Jesus spotted a woman who was crippled so badly she could not stand erect. Modern medicine might view her condition as a chronic sprained back, but the divinity of Jesus rightly discerned the woman's wounded spirit. Even today, humanity's affliction and infirmity are a fertile testing ground for the faithful in need of Jesus' healing.

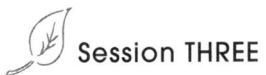

Session THREE

A Prayer to Find the Way

O Jesus, healer of my soul,
sometimes it feels as if
I am like the woman
weighed down
and wounded in spirit.
I ask you to set me free of my
affliction—
the heavy burden of mourning.
Amen.

Steps Along the Path

Worry commonly accompanies grief. Uncertainty about the future may make you wonder whether you can handle life without your loved one. So many plans and dreams wrap around a relationship. Feeling uneasy or apprehensive is a normal emotional response to such a loss. The peace you seek, however, goes beyond feelings. It is rooted in the soul.

In the scripture story, the woman's ailment seemed physical in nature, but it required spiritual healing. As a person of faith, she joined in communal worship and most likely had prayed for God's help for many years. Jesus also must have prayed with the congregation before healing her.

When he saw the crippled woman, he addressed her and declared that she was set free of her problem. Scripture doesn't share her thoughts. Did she realize that her prayer was answered? Was she listening to Jesus? Was she deaf to his voice?

Jesus laid his hands on her, touching her with the Holy Spirit, which brings wholeness to body, mind, heart, soul, will, intellect, and emotion. Jesus, the first charismatic healer of the Church, showed the woman and all humanity his saving power.

 Reflection

The woman's response was dramatic! She immediately stood up straight and glorified God! Can you imagine how she must have felt? Did she dance about and shout? Did she laugh or cry? Did she embrace the Lord or fall at his feet?

What would you do in her situation? What do you do when Jesus touches your sorrow?

Session THREE

 Journal Entry

The crippled woman found a solution to her problem at an unexpected moment. God seems to work that way. Write to Jesus about what cripples your spirit these days and get ready for a reply.

Moving Forward

When you reflect on your spiritual growth during mourning, it helps to consider how Christlike you are in carrying your cross.

Sometimes sorrow makes it difficult to pray and listen to God's message. Normal grief can bring a variety of confusing reactions, such as sadness, anger, anxiety, guilt, and self-reproach. These feelings may foster everyday faults (venial sins) that weaken spiritual health. The sacrament of penance/reconciliation is a powerful way to seek healing.

When you welcome peace, serenity of conscience, and spiritual consolation through the sacrament, God touches you. So stand erect in faith and glorify him!

Closing Prayer

O healer of my soul,
with grateful heart,
I receive the gifts of your Church
and the sacraments that bring me
ever closer to you.
Thank you for guiding
me toward health of body, mind, and
spirit.
Amen.

Session FOUR

Guidepost: Path to Inner Healing

Theme of the fourth session:

Blinders to Faith

Scripture: Luke 18:35–43

Marking the Route

Exercise:

- Take time to think about the scene from scripture and what strikes you most about the story.
- Take about ten minutes to write a letter to God in the space provided. Ask him for something that will help you get through the grieving process.

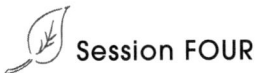 **Session FOUR**

Notes

Home Journal: Path to Inner Healing

Looking Back: *Blind Faith*

The story in Luke 18:35–43 opens as Jesus and a group of followers approached the town of Jericho nestled in the oasis of the Jordan Valley.

A blind man begging by the roadside wondered what was happening and questioned the strangers passing by. When he learned that Jesus of Nazareth was near, he shouted out and begged Jesus to have mercy on him. In a protective reaction that the disciples resorted to time and again, those walking in front rebuked the man and insisted that he be silent. Could these disciples be the Twelve?

The blind beggar called out all the more, addressing Jesus as the Son of David. The title indicated his belief that Jesus was the Messiah—the one anointed by God's Spirit. The Covenant of the Hebrew people was known to have several anointed ones of the Lord, particularly King David, who lived about 1,000 years before Jesus. The Israelites, such as the blind beggar, hoped in the coming of a king, a son of David, who would bring salvation.

The blind beggar's shouts drew Jesus' attention. The Lord stopped and had the crowd bring the blind man forward, involving them in the miracle about to unfold. Surely, Jesus knew what the man wanted, but he asked the man to get more specific than "have mercy on me." How

Session FOUR

often in your grief have you sought Jesus' help and forgotten to be specific?

A Prayer to Find the Way

O compassionate Savior,
I am in need of your pity, too.
Sometimes I'm left by the roadside as
life passes by,
and I do not know that you are near.
Be the Lord of my life,
and I will no longer be blind.
Amen.

Steps Along the Path

When pain of losing someone consumes every waking thought, it debilitates as surely as the blindness the beggar endured. Much can be learned from the beggar's attitude. Notice that once Jesus spoke to him, the man addressed him as "Lord," which acknowledges Jesus' transcendence and dominion over humanity.

We can only wonder if Jesus chose this humble soul at this particular point on the way to Jerusalem to show his disciples what blind faith accomplishes. The message is the same today.

Reflection

Jesus fulfilled one of the characteristics of being the Messiah by bringing good tidings to the afflicted beggar who was blind. He also was sent to bind up the brokenhearted.

Have you called upon the Lord's mercy to gain healing yet? Have you begged? According to the dictionary, a beggar is simply a person who lives by asking for gifts.

Session FOUR

Journal Entry

God knows and provides for your every need. Yet, Jesus sought the beggar's input and granted his wish. Take time to think about what would ease the pain of your grief and explain it to Jesus in the space below.

Moving Forward

Scripture gives us only a peek at some of Jesus' compassionate acts. He never seemed to mind interruptions or being approached by complete strangers. A walk down a country road held stories that inspire the ages.

This week, be inspired. Look for an opportunity to help someone in need of compassion. If you want to imitate our Lord, expect him to put someone needy in your path. Just keep your eyes open!

Closing Prayer

> Dear Lord,
> your consolation gives me
> the strength
> to get beyond my sorrow.
> Thank you for the opportunity to
> grow in spirit this week.
> Amen.

Session FIVE

Guidepost: Way of Suffering

Theme of the fifth session:

His Wounds

Scripture: 1 Peter 2:20b–24

Marking the Route

Exercise:
Observe the wounds of Christ on display. Think about their meaning for you during mourning. Write to him about what comes to mind.

Note: Next week, please bring something to show to the group that reminds you of the faith of your loved one.

Session FIVE

Notes

Home Journal: Way of Suffering

Looking Back: *Christ's Example*

People have always needed reassurance in times of suffering. The passages from Peter's letter (1 Pt 2:20b–24) to members of the early church explore suffering in light of Jesus' example. The Lord's phenomenal courage was worthy of imitation back then and is just as important today. It models how faithful followers confront trials of all kinds—including mourning a loved one.

Peter's letter tells us to be like Jesus: place God's will first and accept that suffering fosters spiritual growth. Yet who greets a painful turn of events with open arms? Not most of us. We feel betrayed. We grumble. We are more human than holy.

When you suffer a loss without complaint, Peter's writing suggests that such patience is a grace before God. God has given you the ability to respond to his call to new life in him (salvation). This favor of God is not earned or deserved; it's a gift.

Session FIVE

A Prayer to Find the Way

O suffering Savior,
you so loved the world
that you chose to suffer and die out
of love for us.
One day we will be with you in a
place that knows no sorrow.
Be my faithful companion on the
road of mourning.
Amen.

Steps Along the Path

The scripture passage reminds us of the call to follow in Jesus' footsteps. Yet the emotions of grieving often bring out the worst in us.

When someone you love dies, you may wrestle with regrets or missed opportunities. You may beat yourself up over the past or simply feel that life beat you up. Do you wonder if you did something to deserve the pain? That's normal. Feeling guilty is a manifestation of grief.

Remember that bad things do happen to good people. Jesus himself faced unthinkable trials, but his response was love. The benevolence of our God was revealed through him.

🍃 Reflection

When Mother Teresa of Calcutta was called a "living saint," she would smile knowingly. She saw God in everyone, but especially in those who suffer.

Think about your departed loved one and how his or her life reflected God to you and others.

Journal Entry

Jesus handled the trials that came his way. He was sinless and honest, returned no insults, accepted suffering, submitted himself to judgment, and obeyedGod's will.

When have you followed in his footsteps on your road of suffering? Write to Jesus about your situation.

Moving Forward

Sorrow can weaken your body, emotional outlook, and spirit, but don't despair. Food strengthens the body and attitude, while the Eucharist strengthens the spirit.

Christ is present in the Blessed Sacrament. It is a sacred sign of grace that Christ wants to share with you.

If you attend Mass and receive the Eucharist as often as possible, expect your life to change. Through communion with Jesus, you learn to truly love God, let go of your miseries, and grow stronger in faith. You will sense his desire to console you in your grief. The saints have testified to this, as do everyday Catholics who receive communion frequently.

The next time you receive the Eucharist, ask Jesus to give you courage in these troubled times.

Closing Prayer

O Jesus,
you are the source of all consolation.
I am grateful to discover you in the
midst of my suffering.
Let me receive you in the Eucharist
with an open heart
and trust completely in you.
Amen.

Session SIX

Guidepost: Final Destination

Theme of the sixth session:

Do Not Weep

Scripture: Luke 7:11–17

Marking the Route

Exercise:

Show the group something that reminds you of the faith of your departed loved one and tell why it is special to you.

Seasons of Hope has four different seasons. Find out when the next one starts.

Session SIX

Notes

Home Journal: Final Destination

Looking Back: *No Tears*

The final scripture reading of this season (Lk 7:11–17) testifies to the power of Jesus to change lives even when hope seems lost. Accompanied by his disciples and a large crowd, Jesus was on the way to a city about five miles southeast of Nazareth. At the city gate, they met a funeral procession of impressive size.

Throughout history, Jewish people have attached great importance to the burial of a loved one. Scripture identifies the bereaved as a widow—a noteworthy point in light of her son's death. If she had no other children, she would have been without support and left to the charity of the community.

The tears of the grieving widow touched the Lord's heart, and he was moved with pity for her. We can only guess what he was thinking. Did he foresee the plight of his own mother before his eyes? Or did he envision this one widow as the embodiment of all those who grieve?

Jesus also attended to the deceased son, who sat up in the coffin at the Lord's command. Jesus didn't stop at restoring the young man's life: he freed him from the coffin and gave him to his mother. The reaction of everyone, including the reunited family, was awe and praise of God.

Session SIX

A Prayer to Find the Way

O compassionate Savior,
you know the needs
of those who mourn.
You don't want us to waste our tears.
Help me recognize
that my loved one has been saved
in your promise of eternal life.
Amen.

Steps Along the Path

You probably have met someone who refuses to attend funerals. His or her fear isn't the same fear (awe of God) that seized the crowd in the scripture story. Often the individual fears the reality and finality of death in general. Some are afraid to express thoughts and feelings about the deceased. Others let their absence make a statement about their relationship with the deceased or bereaved family.

On the other hand, Jesus is ever present to those who mourn. The story about the raising of the widow's son is but one example of his mercy. Today he embraces the brokenhearted through his Church and its funeral rites.

Reflection

Thinking about the funeral or memorial service of your loved one may still bring tears to your eyes, but it is worth contemplating. Compare the emotions displayed during the funeral procession in the gospel to what you experienced.

Journal Entry

Whether or not you were physically present to your loved one at the time of his or her death, you remember your last moments together. Write to Jesus about how he touched those moments or memories.

Session SIX

Moving Forward

If Jesus hadn't brought the young man back to life, the widow would have observed the Jewish customs that dictate distinct periods of mourning. Special observances would have been conducted the first week. A certain prayer that affirms faith in the wisdom of God's decree would have been recited daily. A memorial service would have been held on the thirtieth day and a general period of mourning would have lasted for eleven months.

Our Church also remembers its faithful. In some parishes, it is common for a Mass intention to be offered a month after the funeral. Although Mass intentions can be arranged at any time, those who die within the year are often honored at a communal remembrance celebration in November.

Request that a Mass be celebrated in memory of your loved one. Jesus will be there.

Closing Prayer

O merciful Jesus,
you comfort me in moments of
sorrow and weeping.
Thank you for once again
wiping away my tears.
Amen.

Appendix

Helpful Resources

BOOKS

Chatman, Delle, and William Kenneally. *The Death of a Parent: Reflections for Adults Mourning the Loss of a Father or Mother.* Chicago: ACTA, 2001.

Chilson, Richard. *Prayer: Exploring a Great Spiritual Practice.* Notre Dame, IN: Ave Maria, 2006.

Curry, Cathleen. *When Your Spouse Dies.* Notre Dame, IN: Ave Maria, 1990.

Dawson, Ann. *A Season of Grief: A Comforting Companion for Difficult Days.* Notre Dame, IN: Ave Maria, 2002.

Felber, Marta. *Finding Your Way After Your Spouse Dies.* Notre Dame, IN: Ave Maria, 2000.

Gilbert, Richard B. *Finding Your Way After Your Parent Dies: Hope for Grieving Adults.* Notre Dame, IN: Ave Maria, 1999.

Guntzelman, Joan. *God Knows You're Grieving: Things to Do to Help You Through.* Notre Dame, IN: Ave Maria, 2001.

Hamma, Robert M. *In Times of Grieving: Prayers of Comfort and Consolation.* Notre Dame, IN: Ave Maria, 2004.

Hickman, Martha Whitmore. *Healing After Loss: Daily Meditations for Working Through Grief.* New York: Avon Books, 1994.

Huntley, Theresa M. *Helping Children Grieve: When Someone They Love Dies.* Minneapolis: Augsburg Fortress, 2002.

Lafser, Christine O'Keeffe. *An Empty Cradle, A Full Heart: Reflections for Mothers and Fathers After Miscarriage, Stillbirth or Infant Death.* Chicago: Loyola Press, 1998.

Lambin, Helen Reichert. *The Death of a Husband: Reflections for a Grieving Wife.* Chicago: ACTA, 1999.

Appendix

O'Brien, Mauryeen. *Lift Up Your Hearts: Meditations for Those Who Mourn*. Chicago: ACTA, 2000.

Rupp, Joyce. *Praying Our Goodbyes*. Notre Dame, IN: Ave Maria, 1988.

———. *The Cup of Our Life: A Guide for Spiritual Growth*. Notre Dame, IN: Ave Maria, 1997.

———. *Your Sorrow Is My Sorrow: Hope and Strength in Times of Suffering*. New York: Crossroad, 1999.

Stillwell, Elaine. *The Death of a Child: Reflections for Grieving Parents*. Chicago: ACTA, 2004.

Vogt, Robert. *The Death of a Wife: Reflections for a Grieving Husband*. Chicago: ACTA, 1997.

Wezeman, Phyllis Vos, and Kenneth R. Wezeman. *Finding Your Way After Your Child Dies*. Notre Dame, IN: Ave Maria, 2001.

Woods, Margolyn, and Maureen MacLellan. *Comfort for the Grieving Heart*. Notre Dame, IN: Ave Maria, 2002.

Zonnebelt-Smeege, Susan J., and Robert De Vries. *Getting to the Other Side of Grief: Overcoming the Loss of a Spouse*. Grand Rapids, MI: Baker Books, 1998.

WEB SITES

www.aarp.org/families/grief_loss/ has basic grief information from the AARP, 601 E St., Washington, DC 20049. 888-687-2277.

www.avemariapress.com has books on prayer, bereavement, and spiritual enrichment that comfort the downhearted.

www.bereavementmag.com connects to *Living With Loss Magazine: Hope and Healing for the Body, Mind, and Spirit*.

www.compassionatefriends.com has information and support for families who lose a child.

www.grieflossrecovery.com is a support site with related links.

www.griefwork.org offers pamphlets, books, videos, links to resources, and information on the National Catholic Ministry to the Bereaved, PO Box 16353, St. Louis, MO, 63125. 314-638-2638.

www.griefsong.com has unique ways to honor the death of a loved one.

www.widownet.com has information and self-help resources for, and by, widows and widowers.

Network Directory

Interacting with others of faith who understand what it means to lose a loved one gives you a chance to give and receive support. Use the space below for contact information of participants in your *Seasons of Hope* group.

Name_____

Phone Number_____

E-mail_____

Name_____

Phone Number_____

E-mail_____

Name_____

Phone Number_____

E-mail_____

Appendix

Name_____

Phone Number_____

E-mail_____

Name_____

Phone Number_____

E-mail_____

Name_____

Phone Number_____

E-mail_____

Name_____

Phone Number_____

E-mail_____

Guide to Group Etiquette

A facilitator guides the faith sharing process by keeping the focus on the Lord and the questions. A facilitator doesn't teach, preach, or advise. He or she creates a safe place for you to talk about your feelings about loss and receive consolation.

You are expected to:

- come each week and make it known if you can't
- arrive on time
- treat others with respect
- share your faith story and then let others talk
- be a good listener
- keep what is shared in confidence
- be open to God touching you through others

Don't worry if tears flow. They are part of grieving. Smiles and laughter are welcome, too.

Appendix

Season Three Survey

Please take a few moments to complete the sentences below. Thank you!

1. I learned about *Seasons of Hope* from

2. I think the meeting room is

3. Our meeting time is

4. The length of the weekly sessions is

5. The focus on prayer, scripture, and God is

6. Private time to write, listen to music, or read allows me to

7. I find faith sharing

8. The fellowship aspect of the program is

9. *Participant Journal* homework helps me

10. What I learned from *Seasons of Hope* is

11. When the next *Seasons of Hope* group forms, I

12. I'd also like to say

Date: _____

Name (optional): _____

Acknowledgments

My heartfelt thanks to all who helped shape the *Seasons of Hope Guidebook* and *Participant Journals,* particularly the clergy, friends, family, and bereaved who believe as I do that this work will enrich our parishes.

Sacred Heart Church of Hopedale, Massachusetts, hosted the first version of the bereavement group in the 1990s. Father Daniel R. Mulcahy, Jr. and Father Raymond M. Goodwin welcomed the ministry, Joe and Barbara Grillo helped out, and many enjoyed the sessions and asked for more.

Seasons of Hope in its present form was launched at Sacred Heart Church in Medford, Oregon, in 2004. Much refining was done thanks to my teammates and friends, Father Liam Cary and Mary Murphy who facilitated the sessions with me, and Kathy Wallis and Barbara Halvorsen who joined the team later. Special thanks also to Marie Carnegie, Cliff Downey, Joyce Farrell, Eleanor Geddes, Barbara Halvorsen, Doug Howat, Carol King, Joan Linkogle, Kathy Mannino, Marjorie Moore, Helen Puccetti, Annabelle Roberts, Sharon Roberts, and Arnold Widmer who gave valuable feedback on the program and *Participant Journal* pages they received each week. Some shared the journals with friends and family near and far, a testament to their appeal.

The enthusiasm and expertise of the Ave Maria Press professionals are greatly appreciated, especially those of Eileen Ponder, Bob Hamma, and Keri Suarez. Special thanks also to manuscript readers Linda Bowman, Dione and Larry Callahan, Meganne and Colt Duckworth, Nancy Mann, Helen Pride, and Barbara Wasnewsky for practical suggestions, and Mary Murphy and Sister Mary Pat Naumes for an eye to spiritual matters and Church doctrine.

My husband Bryan's wisdom, love, and generous spirit greatly influenced this work. I treasure the input of our daughter, Meganne, who remains a constant source of love and support, and the memory of dear Erynne whose death opened my heart to all who mourn.

M. Donna MacLeod, RN, MSN, a certified bereavement specialist and hospice professional, began *Seasons of Hope* support groups in 1990. Inspired by the loss of her youngest daughter, Erynne, and the compassionate response of her parish in New England, MacLeod felt called to minister to those who mourn.

A seasoned lecturer and facilitator, MacLeod has organized parish bereavement ministries across the country. She now volunteers for the Diocese of Orlando. A member of the local chapter of the Association for Death Education and Counseling, she also serves on the Board of Trustees for the National Catholic Ministry to the Bereaved.

She was motivated to write *Seasons of Hope Guidebook* by participants in the Oregon Seasons of Hope program who mentioned how beneficial they felt her materials could be to friends and family around the country.

MacLeod enjoys motherhood, grandparenthood, and residing in Florida and on Cape Cod with husband, Bryan. She can be reached through seasonsofhope@cfl.rr.com.